# Mindfulness

# Mindfulness

Gill Hasson

National Trust

# Contents

# Introduction

A student, new to mindfulness, approached the teacher and asked: 'How is it that you are always so calm, relaxed and unhurried? Even when there's confusion and disorder around you, you're not stressed. What's your secret?'

The teacher answered: 'It's very simple; when I walk, I walk, when I eat, I eat, when I listen to someone, I listen to them, when I work, I work. That's all there is to it'.

The student said: 'But I'm doing the same; when I walk I walk, when I eat I eat…'

The teacher replied: 'That's not quite true. When you walk, you think about your work. When you work, you think about the weekend. At the weekend, you think about work. When you're listening to someone you're thinking about what you are going to say. And on it goes. Whatever you do, you are not really there, your mind is

somewhere else and that's why you are missing out on life, that's why calm and happiness slips away from you'.

Being mindful means being aware of and engaged with the here and now, to everyday life, to daily activities such as eating and walking, to your interactions with other people; at work, at home, in your social life and leisure time. Being mindful is being present. It's being aware of what's happening right now.

It's easy to be unaware of what's really going on within you and around you; to be oblivious to your surroundings and other people, and to end up living in your head, caught up in your thoughts without being aware of how those thoughts are taking you away from the present.

Too often, we let the present slip away; it's easy to waste 'now' time, missing what's happening in the only moment that really exists. Mindfulness is a way of living your life so that you are in the present moment more often. It involves bringing your awareness back from the future (the things you worry about that might happen) or the past (the things you wish had or hadn't happened) and into the present moment.

## About this book

Each chapter of this book focuses on one aspect of mindfulness. Each aspect is interrelated – intrinsic to the other aspects of mindfulness. This means, for example, that being **non-judgemental** also involves having a **beginner's mind**. Or that having **patience** involves

being **accepting**. And that accepting means being **non-judgemental**. And so on.

As you read through this book, you'll see that mindfulness is easily practiced by turning everyday activities into opportunities for mindfulness. There are plenty of ideas, as well as advice and tips on how to do this. And, each time you use one of these opportunities to raise your awareness, to **focus**, **engage** or be **patient**, for example, you develop a more whole experience of mindfulness itself. You're making the most of now.

As George Harrison once said: 'It's being here now that's important. There's no past and there's no future … all there is ever, is the now'.

# Beginner's Mind

Begin doing what you want to do now.
We are not living in eternity. We have
only this moment, sparkling like a star in
our hand, and melting like a snowflake.

FRANCIS BACON

# Beginner's mind

Usually, what we do and
how we think is based on
our past experiences, thoughts and
beliefs. We think about things, ourselves and other people
the same way as we've always thought about them, and
we do things in the same way as we always have.

But thinking and doing things in the same old ways
keeps us out of the present and forces us to live in the
past. Responding to other people, situations and events
in familiar, established ways limits how we act in, and
respond to, the world around us. It makes it likely that
we'll miss out on all sorts of possibilities and discoveries,
new ideas and ways of seeing and understanding.

It's different for young children. Experiencing so many
things for the first time, they approach even the most
ordinary of events with interest and curiosity. For them,

every day brings learning and surprises. How might our own life be different if we let go of our preconceptions?

Rather than thinking and behaving in ways that are based on the past, a **beginner's mind** encourages you to start afresh and to respond to things as they are right now, in the present. With a **beginner's mind** you free yourself from your assumptions, expectations and preconceived ideas about someone or something and you engage with other people, events, objects and activities as if for the first time.

The more you approach life with a **beginner's mind**, the more you will experience life in the present moment.

# Standing meditation

*Qigong* (pronounced 'chee-gung') is a Chinese practice that tunes and integrates the body, breath and mind so that they are in harmony with one another. Although there are many styles of *qigong*, they are all based on a standing meditation – *Zhan Zhuang* – which means 'standing like a tree'. This standing meditation is a simple practice you can use to start your day.

## Tuning your body

Stand with your feet shoulder-width apart. Imagine your feet rooted to the ground like a tree. Use a minimum effort to stand but stand tall.

Now, hold your left hand in your right hand, and place both hands on your abdomen. As you breathe in and out your hands will feel your belly moving and enable you to focus on your breath more easily.

## Tuning your breath

Breathe in and out though your nose. Just allow the air to enter and leave effortlessly; slow, long and continuous.

## Tuning your mind

Once your posture is balanced and your breath is calm, your mind can become calm; thoughts can settle by themselves in harmony with your posture and breathing.

Stand like this for a minute or two, for as long as is comfortable and for you to feel present in your body, connected with the Earth, and to feel calm, centred and balanced.

Now, approach your day as a beginner.

Not only can a standing meditation be used to start your day, it can be used whenever you feel the need to ground yourself, feel more balanced and to start again with a **beginner's mind**.

# The tale of the overflowing teacup

A student comes to a Zen master and asks for instruction in the way of Zen Buddhism.

The master begins to explain that Zen emphasises the value of meditation and intuition rather than ritual worship or study of scripture. In an attempt to impress him the student interrupts the master and says, 'Oh, I already know that.'

The master then invites the student to have some tea.

When the tea is ready, the master pours the tea into a teacup, filling it to the brim, spilling tea over the sides of the cup and onto the table.

The student exclaims, 'Stop! You can't pour tea into a full cup'.

The master replies, 'Return to me when your cup is empty'.

The moral of the
story is, of course, that a
**beginner's mind** is empty.
It holds no preconceived
ideas about what
is or what isn't.
It is open and
receptive to
the possibility
of new ideas and
new ways.

# Doing
# something new

When did you last do something for the first time?
Good things can happen when you make the effort
do something new, with a **beginner's mind**. Here are
some ideas:

- Take a different route from
  the one you would usually take
  to work or to visit family
  and friends. Doing
  this encourages you
  to be more **aware**
  and to notice new things for the
  first time. You can even try this at
  the supermarket; if you have
  a particular route that you

normally take around the aisles, change it. Yes, it may slow you down, but you never know what new foods and products you might discover along the way!

- Visit a place that you've never been to. Walk around a part of your town that you've not explored, or take a country walk on footpaths you've not walked before.
- Try a new food or prepare a new dish for dinner.
- Watch a film or a TV series that you know nothing about – you've read no reviews or heard anyone talk about it.
- Do something brave: go on a rollercoaster or hold a spider. Go to a restaurant that is different from the ones you might usually choose. If you usually go with other people, go on your own. Go and see a film by yourself.
- Try a new activity: a dance class, yoga or tennis. Try canoeing or paddle boarding. Learn a new language, to play a musical instrument or any other skill where you start as a beginner.

Experience more of what life has to offer; do something new, for the first time!

# Awareness and acknowledgement

As well as encouraging us to have a **beginner's mind** – to be more **aware** and experience things anew – mindfulness also encourages us to **acknowledge** and appreciate the world around us.

Are there objects, places, people, activities or situations that are so familiar that you no longer notice them or appreciate their worth and value in your life? After the initial thrill of acquiring something or being able to do something for the first few times, the good feelings have worn off. Now, you simply take it for granted; you give it little thought, you assume you'll always have it or be able to do it. But you *can* be more mindful.

Choose three objects in your home. Remember how you felt when you acquired each one. Remind yourself of what it was about each object that you found useful or that you liked or that made you happy.

Now think of something you can do. Can you, for example, remember when you first learnt to ride a bike; how thrilled and excited you were with your newly acquired skill.

The more you pause to be **aware** of, **acknowledge** and appreciate what you can do and what you have, the less you will be reaching for the next thing and the more in the moment you become.

# Being aware
# of nature

The elements of the natural world – the trees and plants,
the animals, the hills and mountains, rivers and other
features of the Earth – offer so much for your senses
to be **aware** of, to **acknowledge** and appreciate.

Feeling the warmth of the sun on your face,
recognizing the smell of recent rain, watching the wind
blow through the trees, sensing the power of the sea,
gazing at the enormity of a star-filled sky; these are
the kinds of moments in
which we can easily
experience being
connected to
and part of
something

bigger, more eternal
than both the physical
and ourselves.

Nature connects the
past, present and future. It
can anchor you and give
perspective; enable you to be
**aware** of where you are and
how you are connected to the greater scheme of things.

There is so much to be **aware** of. Step back to look at
the big picture: the hills and valleys; the landscapes and
the views; the rivers and seascapes. Look at the small
details – a leaf, a flower, a blade of grass, a shell, a feather,
an insect, a spider's web. Examine them in greater detail.
Look for colours, patterns and symmetry.

Be **aware** that nature doesn't just exist in the
countryside, parks and gardens. It is all around, in the
streets and buildings in the towns and cities. Listen, for
example, to the birds, or look for the grass and moss
growing through the cracks in the pavement. Wherever
you are, nature is always there.

# Gratitude

Much of life is made up of small things and fleeting moments. You feel gratitude when you are **aware** of and **acknowledge** those things.

At any one time, when you appreciate what is good in your life, you will receive a positive feeling of connection with the world around you. And during difficult and challenging times when you feel sad, worried or afraid, being **aware** of and **acknowledging** the good things, when and where they exist, can help comfort you. Even if you get to the end of the day feeling that not much has gone right, gratitude helps you see that whatever the difficulties, there were, in fact, some things that made it all worthwhile.

At the end of each day, identify three good things that have happened during that day. You might want to write them down in a notebook or you might simply reflect on what those things are, for instance, while you're getting ready for bed.

Get in the habit of noticing, and reflecting on, the small pleasures – what was good and what went well during the course of that day. It could simply be that you experienced the smell of freshly cut grass, that the sun shone, or that you had a chat on the phone with a friend.

Make a point of looking for things to appreciate. After a while, it will become second nature and you'll end each day knowing that good things did happen.

# Kindness and compassion

When you look for opportunities to be kind, you're
making an effort to be **aware** and to **acknowledge**
in the most positive of ways. You may feel you have
little to offer, but whether it's a smile or a cup of tea,
an offer of your help, or inviting someone to join you
to do something fun, it is the act of giving itself that is
important, not the size of the kindness.

In fact, there are often times when you don't even
have to do something to be kind, you only need
to say something, to
give a compliment.
Like kindness, a
compliment is
mindful because to
give a compliment
you have to be **aware**

and **acknowledge** – to actively
look for and comment on –
other people's efforts and good
intentions. Try to be more **aware**
of what other people do. Tell them
what you noticed and how they
made a positive difference. It could be
someone who serves you in a shop or café, or a person
who provides a service. **Acknowledge** their efforts;
make a positive comment about their work or business.

As well as kind gestures and compliments, you
can raise your **awareness** even further by being
compassionate.

Compassion requires you to be **aware** of and
provide help or support to someone who has
suffered misfortune, or who is stressed and struggling.

Whether it is a gesture of your time or money, or
a smile, a kind word or a supportive comment, being
mindful of the needs of others and reaching out to do
something to support them helps make the world a
better place.

The world needs more kind and compassionate
people. You can be one of them.

# Focus and Engagement

What is this life if, full of care,

We have no time to stand and stare.

No time to stand beneath the boughs

And stare as long as sheep or cows.

**W.H. DAVIES**

# What it means to be focused and engaged

The Buddhist monk and peace activist Thich Nhat Hanh said 'Mindfulness must be **engaged**. Once there is seeing, there must be acting. Otherwise, what is the use of seeing?'

What did he mean by this? The answer is simply that as well as being aware and acknowledging, we need to **engage** with life, to participate and be fully involved in our lives.

Too often, as we go about our day, we're too easily interrupted and distracted. **Engaged** living means managing your attention so that it is **focused** and **engaged** with immediate experience. **Engaged** living means interacting with life more fully. It means making a meaningful connection with everyday activities – cooking and eating, walking, talking and interacting with other people – that are part of all our lives.

# Finding flow

Think of the times you've been so absorbed in what
you were doing that time passed without you realizing:
it could've been a book, a film or a piece of music that
engrossed you. Or perhaps it was a jigsaw puzzle, a
game, a musical instrument or a sport you were playing.
Maybe it was singing in a choir or dancing to music.
Whatever it was, as you did it, no other thoughts entered
your mind because you were completely **focused** and
**engaged** in what you were doing; you didn't even
notice the time that was passing.

When you're doing something that keeps you effortlessly **focused** and **engaged**, you are experiencing something known as 'flow'. When you're in a state of flow, it is as though a water current is carrying you along. Your awareness merges with what you're doing and you are completely 'in the moment'. Your thoughts are positive and in tune with what you're doing.

The level of **engagement** absorbs you deeply and holds your attention. Your mind doesn't wander, it is fully occupied, nothing can distract you.

What do you like doing? Which activities can you **engage** with for ten minutes or immerse yourself in for an hour or more? Identify the things you enjoy doing: hobbies, sports, interests. Know that when you need to bring together your mind, body and environment for a period of time that keeps you present, these are the activities with which you can easily experience flow.

# Take a photo

One way to experience 'flow' – to be fully **focused** and **engaged** with what you're experiencing in the present moment – is by performing a specific creative activity such as drawing, painting or photography. These days, if you're like most of us, your smart phone is always with you. So whether you're indoors or outside, in an open space, or in a town or city, photography is a convenient way to **focus** and **engage** with where you are and what is happening.

Before you take a photo, take a good look around you. What do you see? What do you notice about the patterns, the light, the size and the arrangement of things? Look at the people, the buildings, the objects, the ground, the sky and the nature around you. What shapes, colours, textures, angles, shadows and reflections capture and hold your attention?

Photography encourages you to be fully absorbed in the moment and to notice details you might otherwise have missed. The digital rectangle acts as a frame, **focusing** your eyes and your mind on an image you can capture with your camera.

Even though you may have looked at something many times before, taking a photo can be like noticing something for the first time, and can help you see the world around you differently or, simply, for what it is. And you can zoom in and see details you might otherwise have missed. When you are being mindful, you are less snap happy; instead, you will **focus** on something for longer, you will be more **engaged** with what is in front of you.

If using your camera makes it easier for you to be more present, why not use it? But know when to stop photographing the moment and just live it!

# Eating
# the seasons

Do you know which fruit and vegetables are in season, where you live, at this moment? Do you know, for example, when chestnuts and chicory, beetroot and blackberries, pears and parsnips are at their best?

Not so long ago, you wouldn't have needed to guess, because seasonal eating was just the way we ate. We ate the produce of the market gardens and fields around us: green veg in spring, berries in summer, fruits in autumn and root vegetables in winter, when they were all naturally at their peak in terms of harvest and flavour.

Nowadays, imports from around the world ensure that the fruit and vegetables on the supermarket shelves are the same throughout the year. But why buy asparagus flown in from the other side of the world, or apples shipped from elsewhere, when for many weeks or months of the year you can feast on fruit and vegetables when they're at their best, supplied by local growers and farmers?

Eating the seasons gives us a way to connect and **engage** with nature's cycles and the passing of time.

Getting to know where your food comes from, who grows it and how this is done, can help you feel more connected to that process. Farmers' markets create communities around food that encourage asking questions, the sharing of knowledge, and **engagement** in our own local environment. You can find out what's in season by going to www.eattheseasons.co.uk and find your local farmers' markets at www.farma.org.uk.

# Five senses
# meditation

Whenever things feel off balance and out of your control, the five senses meditation can connect you immediately with the present moment, allowing you to feel grounded, no matter what's going on around you.

1. Look – really look – around you and notice what you can see. Search for something that you don't normally notice, like something tiny or something up high. Notice colours shapes and patterns.

2. Be aware of something that you can feel. Notice the texture – how rough or smooth, hard or soft, or warm or cold something is.
• Put your hands under running water.
• Take a hot or cool shower.
• Pop some bubble wrap.

3. Breathe in a smell.
- Scented flowers – roses, jasmine and lavender.
- Herbs and spices.
- A scented candle.
- The smoke from an extinguished match.

4. Taste something.
- Bite into a lemon or lime.
- Eat some cornflakes, crackers or crisps; something that has a distinct texture and makes a lot of noise.

5. Listen.
- Listen to music.
- Read something out loud; a poem a song or something from a book.
- Listen to someone else talk – on the radio or podcast.

# Walking
# meditations

Walking and counting meditations can **focus**, **engage** and harmonise your body, breath and mind. You can practice a walking meditation for as little as five minutes, or you may want to walk for an hour. Just walk at the speed and pace that keeps you most **focused** and **engaged** with the physical experience of walking.

## Walking and counting meditation no. 1

Breathe in for three, four, or five steps. Breathe out for the same number of steps.

## Walking and counting meditation no. 2

Walk at your normal pace. When you take your first step, either in your mind or out loud, say 'One'. On the next two steps, say, 'One, two'. For the next three steps, say 'One, two, three'. The next four steps should be 'One, two, three, four' and so on, all the way up to ten. When you reach ten, say 'Ten'. Now start to count backwards, with 'Ten, nine', for the next two steps; 'Ten, nine, eight', for the next three steps and so on. Be aware of the rhythm of the counting. Whenever you lose your concentration, simply go back to one.

Any time spent walking – however short – can be used as a meditation practice and can be fitted into your day quite easily. Even walking from the car into the supermarket can be an opportunity for a minute's walking meditation.

# Volunteer

Would you like to make a positive difference to the world? Then volunteer some of your time, energy and skills to a cause that interests you.

Volunteering provides a sense of **engagement** and purpose. There is a wide range of opportunities; you can, for example, support adults to learn to read or mentor ex-offenders. You can be involved in a

conservation and environmental cause, help at a local animal shelter or visit people who are socially isolated.

Whatever you do as a volunteer, even helping out with the smallest tasks can make a real difference to the lives of people, animals and organizations in need.

Go to www.do-it.org to find volunteer opportunities near you. Or visit www.nationaltrust.org.uk/volunteer. The National Trust always has something exciting happening near you. There you can work as a house volunteer or room guide and you can work alongside expert gardeners or help with conservation work on the coast and in the countryside.

As well as making a positive difference, volunteering is also a good way to **engage** with other volunteers. You can meet and create bonds with people who also want to make a contribution to the lives of others; you have a common cause that provides the opportunity to **engage** with other like-minded people.

# Acceptance
# and
# Letting Go

God, grant me the serenity to accept the
things I cannot change, courage to change
the things I can, and wisdom to know
the difference.

**REINHOLD NIEBUHR**

# The meaning of acceptance and letting go

**Acceptance** means that you understand what has or hasn't happened. **Acceptance** is not the same as tolerance. Tolerance is when you grit your teeth and reluctantly put up with a situation. **Acceptance**, on the other hand, is a state of goodwill and grace; an attitude and approach that is patient and benign.

**Acceptance** doesn't mean that you have to resign yourself to something, to give in. It simply means recognizing that you cannot change what it is that has or hasn't happened, and that right now the situation is what it is. What could be more futile than resisting a state that already exists? With **acceptance**, you **let go**; you don't hold on to thoughts, feelings, situations and events. You understand that they are part of the past.

You *can* move on but before you do, you need to **accept** what has brought you to this present moment. In fact, in what is known as the 'acceptance paradox', **acceptance** is what makes change possible. If you don't **acknowledge** and **accept** what has happened and what is happening, it is difficult to move on. But once you **accept** something, rather than react to it – take opposing action – you can respond to it by acting thoughtfully and favourably.

When you stop dwelling on what could, should or shouldn't have happened, you can then begin to focus on what to do next. The past is gone; the future is not yet here. What exists between past and future is the present moment and it is in the present that **acceptance** occurs.

# Accepting change

We may not know how or when changes will happen in our lives, but one thing is for sure – change *will* happen. Changes are not, however, always welcome. Unwelcome change can mean facing an uncertain future, not knowing what to expect and assuming the worst.

There are some things, like the changes in the weather, that we **accept** are out of our control. But too often we resist change, we cling to the past and fear the future. We try to hold on to people, places and things and we struggle to **let go**.

And yet, even though you might not be able to control a particular change or stop it from happening, you *can* control how you respond to change. Make yourself aware of the positive things, such as new opportunities, that change brings. **Acknowledge** and do what you can to prepare for the difficult aspects

of a change. Then look for and **focus** on the positive aspects.

You can embrace change by seeking change. Deliberately making changes is an effective tactic for coping with the inevitable changes that will occur in your life. For example, you could, if you are able, change how you travel: walk instead of cycle, cycle instead of drive, or take public transport; take the stairs instead of the lift.

Move the clock or bin to a different place in the room. Or move the teabags or plates to a different cupboard in the kitchen. Yes, you will automatically look for these items in the place they used to be, at least to begin with, but not only will you adapt to the changes, having to think about these things each time you go to use them will also make you more aware.

# Accepting sadness and disappointment

We can easily **accept** feelings of happiness and joy, pride and satisfaction when things go well. But when things don't turn out well, when we lose something or someone we love, when we fail to achieve something, when we are let down or a good situation comes to an end – the sorrow, distress and sadness we feel is not so easy to **accept**.

And yet, although it doesn't feel nice, the whole point of sadness is to slow down our body and mind and give us time to absorb the loss or failure; to **accept** that what has happened *has* happened and that nothing can change that.

So, when you're sad, upset, disappointed and distressed, just know that you need to sit with it and to feel it. Allow yourself to be sad; **accept** sadness for what it is – a temporary and useful state that can help you adjust and adapt to different circumstances.

Cry if you feel like it. Crying is cathartic; it helps relieve emotional tension. It unifies your thoughts, feelings and physical body.

Give yourself time but know that rumination – going over and over your feelings of sadness – cannot go on forever. At some point you need to **let go** and move on. And sometimes, that might be in a different direction.

# All things come and go

Let everything happen to you. Beauty and terror. Just keep going. No feeling is final.

RAINER MARIA RILKE

Everything that comes into this world also leaves it. Just as the seasons come and go, so does night and day, sun and rain, health and wealth, war and peace. Nothing is permanent and all eventually passes. Mindfulness can help you to understand this; to appreciate the good, the enjoyable and happy times, to make the most of now, knowing it will not last.

The chocolate meditation is a good way to experience the passing of pleasure. Simply place a piece of chocolate or a toffee into your mouth and as it slowly melts away, be aware of, appreciate and enjoy its texture and flavour.

Just as pleasure doesn't last, neither do difficulties and problems. One way or another, they will pass. Think back to a difficult time, a time when you had a setback, a challenge or a problem to deal with. However long it lasted, it wasn't permanent. One way or another it passed. Things may not have worked out the way you wanted them to, but they didn't remain the same. Like clouds passing in the sky or leaves floating down a stream, things moved on. Remind yourself of this when you are in the middle of a difficult, challenging experience. Remind yourself that, 'This too shall pass'.

# Melting ice-cube meditation

Put a cube of ice on a plate. Then take a minute to be still and centre yourself, bringing your attention to your breathing as it comes in and out. After a minute or so of this – about ten slow, quiet breaths – place the ice cube on the palm of your hand.

Feel the texture of the ice. Watch the ice melt and the water drip through your fingers.

Be aware of your thoughts, your physical sensations, and any emotional response you have. Do you feel a stinging sensation, burning or tingling? Notice what is going through your mind: perhaps you're thinking of how long you'll need to wait until the ice melts; you're hoping it will end soon. Or maybe it's a hot summer day and this feels soothing.

The ice-cube meditation can help you recognise and **accept** the impermanence of mental and physical discomfort and your emotional response to it.

## Hand-squeezing meditation

If you don't have an ice cube, try this:

Make a tight fist with both of your hands at the same time. Breathe in for about ten seconds and tighten your hands as you breathe in. Squeeze tighter. Breathe out and release your hands. Now **focus** on how your hands feel and stay focused for as long as you can or until that feeling goes away.

The hand-squeezing meditation can also help you recognise the impermanence of mental and physical discomfort and your emotional response to it.

# Forgiving

We all know what it feels like to be wronged by someone else; to be deceived or lied to, to be humiliated or let down. When someone does something that upsets or angers you it is not always easy to forgive them. It can feel like you're giving in, absolving the other person, freeing them from blame and letting them get away with it.

But forgiveness is for *your* benefit – for *your* peace of mind – not the person who hurt or offended you. Forgiveness means **letting go** of the distress, resentment

or anger that you feel as a result of someone else's actions. It involves no longer wanting punishment, revenge or recompense. You've already been hurt once, you don't need to let the offence and your pain continue to hurt you by holding onto it. You're not responsible for the other person's actions. But you *are* responsible for yours. You are responsible for your happiness and peace of mind. Understanding this can help you to look at forgiveness in a new light.

Of course, forgiveness can't be forced, you have to be drawn to it. But when you're ready, know that forgiveness *is* possible.

**Acknowledge** and **accept** what happened and how it affected you. You might find it helpful to write an honest, heartfelt letter telling the other person how hurt and angry you are. Then **let go**: crumple up the letter and burn it. As you watch the smoke rise, imagine it carrying your hurt and resentment into the air.

Now change the story you replay to yourself and other to people. Change your story to one that tells of your decision to forgive; to **accept** and learn from what happened, to **let go** and move on.

# Overwhelm

Deadlines at work, colleagues, customers or clients to attend to, things to do at home, friends and family needing your time or attention: too much to do and too little time to do it in. And even when you're not trying to do everything, you're thinking about it. But you can't think clearly.

Does this sound familiar? At one time or another most of us experience busy periods in our lives. You feel stressed and overwhelmed as you think about all the things that need to be done and have yet to be done.

Stop! Stop living in the future. Bring yourself back to the present.

**Acknowledge** and **accept** how you feel and how things are at this moment before thinking about what you can do to manage them. It's a strategic acceptance; you may not like what's happening, but instead of fighting it, by **accepting** that you have a lot to do, you will free your mind to think more clearly.

Everything simply is what it is. You can choose how to interpret it and how to respond. By being aware and acknowledging that you're getting stressed, you can regain control and bring things back to the present moment.

So, the next time you find yourself overwhelmed, say to yourself, 'Be here, now'. Pause. And breathe. Take a few minutes to stop what you're doing and do nothing. Just focus on breathing. A simple two-minute breathing space will help calm you down, re-engage your brain and allow you to collect and clarify your thoughts. You can then move on to thinking about what you are going to do next.

# Letting go of
# what doesn't make
# you happy

Whether it's leaving a job you don't like, calling
time on a friendship that's run its course, ditching the
social-media account that leaves you feeling inadequate
or resentful, or putting down a novel because it's boring,
instead of **letting go** of something that we're not
enjoying, too often, we simply hang on in there.

Of course, it's not always easy to walk away from
something you once enjoyed or that you thought would
be a good idea to be involved with. But refusing to
**let go** of something that's making you miserable means
you are allowing the past to dictate the present.

Life's too short!

Realise that at the time, based on what you knew and how you felt, you *did* make the right choice. At the time, your decision *was* the right one. Now though, the situation isn't right for you. **Accept** that.

**Let go** of the past and begin again in the present.

Are you really going to let new opportunities slip by just because you're too busy holding on to things that don't make you happy? **Let go** of the things you dislike and make room for something better. Think about what you have to gain from the moment you **let go**, rather than what you have to lose by pulling out.

# Being
# Non-judgemental

Be curious, not judgemental.

WALT WHITMAN

# How to be non-judgemental

Being **non-judgemental** means that you don't see something as 'good' or 'bad', 'right' or 'wrong'. Instead, you just observe it or experience it; you don't need to make any sense of a situation, your thoughts, feelings and actions or other people's behaviour. When you're being **non-judgemental** you simply experience things in an objective way; noticing, acknowledging and accepting things as they are, not as you think they should or shouldn't be.

People are just people, events and situations are just events and situations, thoughts and feelings are just thoughts and feelings. None of them are good, bad, right or wrong. They just are what they are.

Being **non-judgemental** doesn't mean that you approve of things that go against your values. Instead, it means moving into a place of acceptance of what is. It is being aware that things are only good or bad, right or wrong if you choose to see them that way.

Imagine wearing a heavy pair of glasses. Imagine these glasses have thick, cracked, cloudy lenses that give a skewed, distorted view of yourself, other people and events. Now imagine taking off the glasses. Blink a few times, take a step back, and really see the world around you, unimpeded by judgement.

# Feed the
# other tiger

Once there lived an old man who kept many different kinds of animals. Two tigers that lived together in one cage particularly intrigued the old man's grandson. The tigers had different temperaments; one was calm and gentle and accepting while the other was unpredictable, mean and aggressive.

'Do they ever fight, Grandfather?' asked the boy.
'Occasionally, yes they do,' admitted the old man.
'And which one wins?'
*'Well, that depends on which one I feed the most'*.

Being able to manage and control how judgemental you are about someone or something depends, in part, on how much you 'feed' your judgement and the emotions that accompany it. No matter who it is and what the situation, there's always more than one way to think about and respond to something or someone.

Keep in mind that being judgemental is like feeding the difficult tiger; it can create conflict and makes things worse.

# Mindful listening

The idea of this exercise in being **non-judgemental** is to listen to some music from a neutral position with a present awareness that's unhindered by preconceived ideas or past experience.

Find a piece of music you've not heard before. You could do this by going to a music-streaming service and picking something at random. Or you could ask someone else to pick something they think you might not have listened to before: folk, blues, jazz, punk, classical or opera.

Try not to get drawn into judging the music by its genre, title or artist name before it has even begun. Instead, just listen. Whether the music is or isn't to your liking at first, let go of your judgement and give acceptance a chance.

Don't think. Don't judge. Just listen.

Try to separate out and listen to the sound of each instrument. Listen to the vocals; the sound of the voice, its range and tones. If there is more than one voice, see if you can separate out each voice.

Don't think. Don't judge. Just listen.

# Being non-judgemental of other people

Do you judge other people?
Do you judge what they say and
what they do? Of course you do. We
all do: we listen to what someone says –
their thoughts, opinions and beliefs; we see something
someone does – the way they live their life perhaps, or
do their work; and if we don't approve, understand or
agree, instead of accepting, we judge and criticise.

It rarely occurs to us that the
other person is simply viewing
or managing a situation in a
different way to us. But you
can be more mindful; you can
be more aware of when you're
being judgemental of other
people. How? Well, if you think

they've brought it on themselves or that
they should change their ways, then you are
judging them. If you are dismissive of a person's
opinions then you are being judgemental. If you talk
disparagingly about them then you are being judgemental.

Remember a judgement you've made about someone
else; perhaps you judged someone for their political
or religious beliefs, the way they dressed, spoke or the
way they did something, or the fact that they didn't do
something; their failings and foibles, weaknesses and
weirdness. Did your judgement
distance you from others or make
you feel more connected?

You can practice viewing other
people's circumstances and choices
with a **non-judgemental** mind;
a **beginner's mind**. Next time you
read or listen – to the radio, TV or to
an overheard conversation in public – and
someone else's opinion irritates you, think about
giving them the benefit of the doubt. What could
be a reasonable explanation for why they've done
or said what they did?

# Letting go of self-judgement

Many of us are familiar with our inner critic: that disapproving voice in our head that is quick to judge and is ready to give us a hard time. But how can we let go of self-judgement and self-blame when we've made a mistake or done something we believe to be wrong?

First, try to become aware of judgements arising in your mind. Whenever you feel guilt or regret, notice the thoughts you have about yourself. More often than not you won't even notice when you're berating and reprimanding yourself. But when you do, ask yourself, 'In what way is it helpful for me to think like this?'

Know that all the time you are unable to forgive yourself for something that happened days, weeks, months or even years ago, you're living in the past; you're letting the hurt and pain burden you by holding onto it.

Think about how you will view your mistake, what you did wrong or failed to achieve a year from now, in two years or five years? That's not to say that you don't take responsibility for whatever you did or didn't do. Taking responsibility means you accept what you did or didn't do. Nothing can change what happened. But what *can* change is what happens next. Learn from it – act differently next time.

Acknowledge that you're continuing to grow into the person you're becoming, and that the person you are right now also deserves kindness.

Then let it go and move on.

# Commentary meditations

### Walking commentary

Plan a five-minute walk – in the park, around the
block, along a footpath, up the road and back again, or
wherever you like. Once you set off, begin a running
commentary in your head describing your walk and
everything you notice. For example: 'I'm opening the
door. I'm leaving the house. I'm shutting the door. I'm
walking down the path and I'm turning left. A car just
drove past. I'm walking past my neighbour's house.
I can hear the birds singing …'

Notice that you are being objective – not influenced by feelings or personal opinion – you are simply describing what you are doing and what you are experiencing; what you see, hear, smell and so on. You are not making judgements. Nothing is good or bad, right or wrong. You are being **non-judgemental**.

## Driving commentary

Make a running commentary when you're driving in your car. Describe out loud what you can see, and what you're doing: 'I'm waiting for the car behind to pass. I'm looking in the mirror. Now I'm turning the steering wheel and I'm turning left. I'm changing gear. I'm passing someone on a bike. I'm changing up to fourth gear'.

Just like a walking commentary, a driving commentary is objective – you're not making judgements – you're simply **focused** and **engaged** with driving your car.

# Mindful chores

Everyday routine tasks, such as loading the dishwasher, washing up, ironing, cooking, cleaning and tidying up, can help challenge your assumptions and judgements about what is an ordeal – a tedious chore – and what is just a series of actions carried out in order to get something done.

It is easy to make all sorts of negative judgements that are not necessary to do the job and get it done. But washing up is just washing up. Doing the laundry is just doing the laundry. Cleaning the bathroom is just cleaning the bathroom. Emptying the bin is just emptying the bin. None of these activities are good or bad. They are just activities. They are only annoying, tedious, boring or something to be resented if you think of them in that way.

So, if household chores like cooking and cleaning seem irritating or boring to you, try doing them as an exercise in mindfulness. Instead of letting the time spent on these things be an unpleasant ordeal, engage yourself with those tasks without judgement.

Just do them without giving them any thought at all.

# Patience
# and Trust

There is more to life than
increasing its speed.

MAHATMA GANDHI

# Allow yourself to be patient

So often, when we realise that something or someone is going to take longer than we'd like, we start looking for ways to hurry things up. We try to get somewhere more quickly, rush an outcome, or make the unknown known. This is when we need **patience**.

Like acceptance, **patience** is the ability and willingness to let something be; to wait calmly without needing to change it to when *you* want it to happen. With **patience,** there is understanding and **trust** that things will develop in their own time; that life is a process of unfolding. With **patience**, you know that there is a time for everything and everything takes time.

In a variety of situations, you may not even be aware that you are being impatient because your mind has already jumped ahead to how and where you want things to be. And even if you *are* aware of being impatient, you might think that the causes of your impatience are events or other people creating the delay. But the cause is in your own mind; it is your reaction that causes impatience, not what is or isn't happening.

Try to recognise when you're becoming impatient. Is your mind calm or agitated? Is your body relaxed or tensed? Stop fuelling your impatience with judgements about how wrong it all is or how slow things are. If you feel yourself becoming agitated, irritated and frustrated, tell yourself, 'This too shall pass'. Time always passes, and how you feel during that time is of your own making. Assume that the delay has occurred because you needed to slow down and reset. Shift your thinking about a delay and you'll arrive with a calmer, clearer mind and a better attitude.

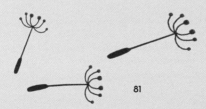

# Gaining
# perspective

Getting a sense of perspective can help you be more
**patient**. Gaining perspective means having a sense of
where you are in the greater scheme of things; taking
everything else into account and understanding the
relative importance of things.

   So often, it is the daily hassles that we get impatient
about. But whatever it was that irked you, when you
look back now – a day, a week
or months later – it seems a lot

less awful; even rather trivial. Perspective helps you to understand that as frustrating as things might be at this moment, the situation *will* change; life will continue and one way or another, things will work out. You might want things to be different in the future, but in the present moment you **accept** things as they are and for what they are.

When there are delays and hold-ups, try not to judge. Instead, stand back, observe and simply describe. Recognise, for instance, 'I am stuck in traffic' or 'The waiter brought me the wrong dish'. The situation is what it is. It only becomes something that frustrates you if you attribute a negative meaning to it.

Practice **patience**; make yourself wait. Next time, rather than choosing the shortest queue, choose the longest queue. Try standing in line and just observing and listening to people around you.

Slow down and experience the unfolding of your life.

# Stone stacking

Next time you're at a pebble beach, find a number of flat stones and create a stone stack. Choose each stone, assess its shape, size and weight, then place them so that they sit on top of one another.

Stone stacking requires awareness, engagement and **patience** as you balance the stones in vertical arrangements.

The engaging process of handling and balancing cool stones is meditative; the process of building the structure brings with it a sense of **patience** and calm.

Although stone stacks look beautiful against a natural backdrop, leave no trace; don't move the stones to a different location but keep them where you found them so that they can naturally break up and be washed away.

Be sure to create your stack of stones above the high-tide line, to avoid disturbing habitats and don't build or leave a stack where it could cause a risk to others, for example on cliffs where it could trip people up in some way.

# Watching and listening to birds

Birds are all around us; they're a part of our everyday life and our experience of nature. If you take just a little bit of time to look out for and listen to birds – in your garden, in parks, allotments, fields, woods and forests, along riverbanks, at the seaside, in your town and city – you'll soon be aware that there's birdlife everywhere.

You don't need much to enjoy birds, just your eyes or ears.

The sounds of many species are characteristic and easy to recognise. You'll already know some birds solely by their sounds: the hoot of an owl, the cry of a seagull, the coo of a pigeon, the call of a cuckoo. Others – a robin, blackbird, blue tit and sparrow – you will easily recognise by sight.

Start bird-watching just by looking out your window or sitting somewhere out in the open – the garden, park or a street bench. Sit **patiently** for a while. Listen. What can you hear? What can you see? Whether it's up in a tree, high in the sky, on the ground or in a bush, it is more than likely that you will notice a bird or two.

Notice details: their colours, their movements and their behaviour. Watch what they do and where they go.

Intrigued? Invite them round to your place; give them food by providing a bird feeder. Be **patient**. It may take time before you get some visitors. www.rspb.org.uk has a wealth of information and advice on feeding and giving birds a home in your garden, patio or balcony.

## To the Cuckoo

O blithe New-comer! I have heard,
I hear thee and rejoice.
O Cuckoo! shall I call thee Bird,
Or but a wandering Voice?

While I am lying on the grass
Thy twofold shout I hear;
From hill to hill it seems to pass,
At once far off, and near.

**WILLIAM WORDSWORTH**

# Patient
# gardening

The proverb 'patience is a virtue' could have been written for gardeners. I started my small garden with a *Kerria japonica* from my Dad's garden, a 6in (15cm) tall *Euonymus japonicus*, an evergreen shrub, from a garden centre, some spring bulbs and a couple of packets of seeds.

I wanted an instant, beautiful established garden but, of course, as experienced gardeners know, nature can't be hurried. Creating a garden takes time and **patience**.

I had to wait for the plants to grow in their own time and for the garden to grow into itself. I've learned, of

course, that with gardening, the pleasure is in the waiting: in accepting and appreciating the progress of each plant, shrub and tree at every stage of its life cycle. Twenty-five years later, my *Euonymus* has slowly grown to be 4ft (1.2m) high, the daffodils continue to flower each spring, and the *Kerria* flowers every April, around the time of my birthday.

The thing with instant gardens is that they are unlikely to possess the same qualities as a garden in which time has been allowed to do its work. Trees, shrubs and plants all need to be able to grow into their space and make it their own.

And as much as nature cannot be hurried, nature is also forgiving. If a shrub is pruned too hard, if seeds are sown but don't germinate, if nasturtiums are plagued by blackfly, then there's always next year. There is no rush, as their time will always come around again. We just have to **trust** and be **patient**.

# Slow food

We've all done it: bolted down our breakfast before racing out of the door; wolfed down a sandwich in our lunch break; or mindlessly eaten a take-away in front of the TV. When life is fast, eating quickly or on the go can become the norm. We shovel food into our mouths without paying much attention to what we're eating and whether or not we feel full. But it doesn't have to be like this!

'Slow food' is about the experience of sourcing, preparing, and enjoying the whole process. The Slow Food movement (www.slowfood.org.uk) was founded as an antidote to the rise of fast food and fast life. It supports the awareness of good food, the enjoyment of eating and a slow pace of life. A life in which meals are not eaten on the run, with little regard for where your food comes from, how it is produced, prepared and consumed.

Slowing down
to cook, eat and
drink intentionally
are part of developing
a healthier relationship with food. It can take your body
up to 20 minutes to register the fact that you are full but
during that time you may be continuing to eat. Slow
down. Put your fork down every few mouthfuls. Check
how you're feeling; ask yourself, 'Am I still hungry, or
am I full?'

You can practice eating more slowly and **patiently**.
Try swapping over your knife and fork while eating
a meal, or using chopsticks. When you take the time
to enjoy your food you're more likely to notice
flavours and textures and be more aware of when
you are full.

# Tea ritual

Tea-making and drinking embraces a number of aspects of mindfulness; each time you make a pot or a cup of tea, you begin again. The process is so simple and familiar you can do it without **judgement**. Making and drinking tea is a way of being present; **focusing**, **engaging** and exercising **patience**.

Like all rituals, the ritual of making and drinking tea – a succession of simple actions carried out in a specific sequence – can help to slow you down and connect you to yourself, to where you are, to the here and now.

So, when things become rushed, pause and make tea.

You could store your tea in a lovely container. Perhaps use a special teapot; one handed down from a parent or grandparent could be the star – the focus – of your tea ritual. Try using loose-leaf tea; use your fingers to scoop out the tea leaves, and feel their size, shape and texture as you drop them into a warmed teapot. Listen to the water – the bubbling and gurgling – as it begins to boil. Watch for the wisps of steam coming from the spout. Listen to the sound of the water as you pour it into the pot or the cup. Look for the change in the colour of the water – the transformation from clear water to tea – as it is poured onto the tea leaves. What aromas rise up in the steam? Are they earthy, floral or fruity? Add the milk and watch the colour change again.

Take a sip of tea. Sit calmly and quietly as you drink it.

Now and again, make a ritual out of making tea. It can slow you down and connect you to the moment. And all with just some water and leaves.

# Index

**Gill Hasson** is a writer and teacher. She runs courses on confidence and self-esteem, assertiveness and resilience. As well as mindfulness, she has written books on kindness, happiness and emotional intelligence.

First published in the United Kingdom in 2019 by
National Trust Books
43 Great Ormond Street
London WC1N 3HZ
An imprint of Pavilion Books Company Ltd

ISBN: 9781911358763

A CIP catalogue record for this book is available from the British Library.

25 24 23 22 21 20
10 9 8 7 6 5 4 3

Reproduction by by Rival Colour Ltd, UK
Printed and bound by Toppan Leefung Printing Ltd, China

This book can be ordered direct from the
publisher at the website: www.pavilionbooks.com,
or try your local bookshop.